What Is God Like?

The Biblical God for Contemporary Man

by
Robert H. Lescelius

Roadbuilding for Revival Series

ISBN 1-56632-100-X

Printed in the United States of America.

Isaiah 57:14-21

And shall say, Cast ye up, cast ye up, prepare the way, take up the stumblingblock out of the way of my people. For thus saith the high and lofty One that inhabiteth eternity, whose name is Holy; I dwell in the high and holy place, with him also that is of a contrite and humble spirit, to revive the spirit of the humble, and to revive the heart of the contrite ones. For I will not contend for ever, neither will I be always wroth: for the spirit should fail before me, and the souls which I have made. For the iniquity of his covetousness was I wroth, and smote him: I hid me, and was wroth, and he went on frowardly in the way of his heart. I have seen his ways, and will heal him: I will lead him also, and restore comforts unto him and to his mourners. I create the fruit of the lips; Peace, peace to him that is far off, and to him that is near, saith the LORD; and I will heal him. But the wicked are like the troubled sea, when it cannot rest, whose waters cast up mire and dirt. There is no peace, saith my God, to the wicked.

What Is God Like?

For thus saith the high and lofty One that inhabiteth eternity, whose name is Holy; I dwell in the high and holy place, with him also that is of a contrite and humble spirit, to revive the spirit of the humble, and to revive the heart of the contrite ones.

—Isaiah 57:15

The state of the Evangelical Church is one of great concern to many in our day. John Seel writes of *The Evangelical Forfeit*.[1] In the culture war we have become a sub-culture, self-enclosed and having no significant impact on the prevailing culture.

Within our own little world and independent of everything else, we have all that we need. We have Christian talk shows, Christian Johnny Carsons, Christian theme parks, Christian night clubs, and Christian comedians. We even have our own T-shirts. As far as the marketing industry is concerned, the Evangelical Church is a whole marketing area within itself.

We come to our little ghettos every Sunday, meet together, and rush home again. We rush back for a little enclave on Wednesday and then quickly back to our homes. We have minimal contact with each other.

When it comes to the matter of statistics, certainly the number of churches is growing, and the number of professing evangelical Christians is increasing. Looking at statistics and polls alone, one would conclude that America is in the millennium compared to other nations of the world. What other country has as many churches,

Christian schools, and seminaries? Yet, these statistics seem to be clouding the fact that underneath all the statistical growth, we are impotent. As far as the culture is concerned, evangelicalism is irrelevant in our day.

One evangelical leader has observed, "We are losing the culture war, not in the public arena, but within the church. Until we renew what it means to be a Christian in the church, we won't have credibility to speak to the world."[2]

As Pogo said, "We have met the enemy, and he is us."

We are, in fact, not even certain of what evangelicalism is today. Seel notes four approaches to defining it:[3]

Doctrinal definition: Evangelicals have been identified by a set of core beliefs. Yet some leaders have argued that as a whole it is not "defined, directed or driven by truth." Pragmatism and mysticism have replaced the authority of Scripture in our day.

Institutional definition: Evangelicalism has become a fraternity of religious organizations, a network of mainly parachurch organizations, like "medieval fiefdoms—superficially friendly but competitive empires that fight for their own expanding turf while professing nominal allegiance to the same distant king."[4]

Shared experiences: Evangelicals are also defined as those who are "born again Christians" or as sharing a charismatic experience. This, however, is an admission of the influence of the world, where "images and feelings replace words and truth."[5]

Functional definition: Behavior, church attendance, Bible reading, prayer, evangelism, etc., are used to identify evangelicals. By polls and statistics evangelicalism is increasing, yet this masks its impotence in cultural influence.

By definition evangelical has to do with the "Evangel," the GOSPEL. Evangelicals are those who believe, proclaim, and practice the gospel of the Lord and Savior Jesus Christ. The message is called the gospel of God, the gospel of Christ, the gospel of grace, the gospel of salvation. Hence it concerns the concepts of God, Christ, grace and salvation—great theological truths. The problem lies in a subtle departure from these foundational truths over the years. The psalmist asked, "If the foundations be destroyed, what can the righteous do?" (Psa. 11:3). We may also ask, "While the foundations were being destroyed, what were the righteous doing?"

David Wells has pinpointed the problem in two books, *No Place for Truth: Whatever Happened to Evangelical Theology?* and *God in the Wasteland: The Reality of Truth in a World of Dreams*.[6] He states that we need a fresh encounter with the transcendent God. The Church has lost its sense of God's sovereignty and holiness.

Seel contends:

> Modern American evangelicals have largely abandoned our historical connection to pre-American evangelicals—to the patristic fathers, the reformers, the Puritan divines, and others. American evangelicals have an American psyche.[7]

The problem is theological. Our theology, or lack of it, will reflect in our worship, methodology and behavior.

Building a Road for Revival

Isaiah 57:14 is a call to build a road (cast ye up), prepare a way, and remove all obstacles from the way of God's people.

The context would lead one to deep despair as to the future of Israel. From Isaiah 56:9 the message Isaiah conveys is one of condemnation of the wicked. Consider these passages in Isaiah:

56:9-12   A call to the Gentiles to destroy Israel.
57:1,2   The death of the righteous will be a blessing, for they will escape the calamity to come.
57:3-10   Israel's false religious practices are exposed and condemned.
57:11-13 Israel's forgetfulness of God is exposed.

Yet verse 14 introduces a promise of salvation! "BUILD A

ROAD," a constructive enterprise. This compares to 40:3,4, where a road is to be built for the LORD to travel to His people, a prophecy fulfilled by John the Baptist, the forerunner of the Messiah.

"Here it is a road that leads to the achievement of God's purposes and is prepared for the people to travel on and thus come to their goal." So comments Leupold.[8] It involves the removal of all obstacles that lie in the way of achieving what God had promised the nation. Remove doubt. Remove littleness of faith. Remove discouragement. Bulldoze them out of the way. The Lord is very near! He is at hand to save, to revive (Isa. 57:15)!

Isaiah 57:15 begins with "for," giving the reason to remove the obstacles. It is evident that one chief obstacle is ignorance of and unbelief relating to the NATURE OF GOD.

WHAT IS GOD LIKE? Our passage is one of the most majestic in the Bible. Surely no carnal man could or would have written such words. By divine inspiration Isaiah tells us that God is a God of Transcendent Majesty and Condescending Mercy.

The God of Transcendental Majesty

For thus saith the high and lofty One that inhabiteth eternity, whose name is Holy; I dwell in the high and holy place (Isaiah 57:15).

The Transcendence of God

The Supreme One
God is said to be . . .

- **High** (Hebrew, *ram*)—high and exalted in Himself alone.
- **Lofty** (*nissa'*)—towering above, transcendent in relation to His creation. This is not speaking in a physical sense of elevation or altitude, but that God is an order of Being beyond and above His creation. The same description is given of Adonay Yahweh in chapter 6:1, the same words being used.
- **Inhabiting eternity**, i.e., He dwells forever. God is a Necessary Being, One Who cannot *not* be, eternal. We are contingent beings, owing our being to God.
- **The Holy One** (*qadôsh*)—separate, different. This applies, first of all, to His separateness from creation, and then to His separateness from all impurity and defilement.

Thus holy days, holy seasons, holy places and holy people are different, because they all have to do with God.

He is the God of exalted MAJESTY.

The Sovereign One

God's sovereignty is established in this verse. The basis of God's sovereignty is threefold:

The Supreme Majesty of God. Because He is holy in the absolute sense, God is supreme in majesty over all His creation, thus He alone rules as King over all time and eternity.

> But our God is in the heavens: he hath done whatsoever he hath pleased (Psa. 115:3).

The Perfection of God. Sovereignty is not an attribute but the divine prerogative. He is the only One Who has the right to rule over everything.

The Creatorship of God. God is the Creator, thus His will is the cause of all things. He is the absolute authority over heaven and earth. Nothing is outside His control.

> Thou art worthy, O Lord, to receive glory and honour and power: for thou hast created all things, and for thy pleasure they are and were created (Rev. 4:11).

God is the only Being in the universe Who has the absolute right and ability to do whatever He pleases. Man, therefore, is responsible to his Creator-King and must answer to Him.

The Holiness of God

He is "the Holy One," Who lives in "the high and holy place."

Holiness defined

Holiness is God's self-affirmed purity. It is that perfection of God in virtue of which He eternally wills and maintains His own moral excellence. The divine will is in absolute harmony with the divine nature.

Holiness is God's central and supreme attribute. It is the hub out of which all the spokes extend. Holiness is a moral attribute which is co-extensive with, and applicable to, everything that can be predicated to God.

For example, we can speak of holy love, holy wrath, holy power, holy wisdom, but we cannot speak of loving wrath. Can you imagine the ark of Noah with a smiley face painted on the hull saying, "Smile, God loves you"?

It is the only attribute exalted to the superlative degree: Holy! holy! holy! (Isa. 6:1-3; Rev. 4:8). Our Lord addressed Him as holy Father, righteous Father, not "loving heavenly Father" (John 17). Though He is indeed the latter, He is absolutely and essentially holy above all.

The holiness of God is active—the primary motive in citing all He does. HOLINESS IS:

- the source and standard of the right—PURITY,
- the free moral movement of God—PURITY WILLED,
- the supreme object of His regard and maintenance— PURITY WILLING ITSELF.

Holiness Displayed

Note several illustrations:

Nadab and Abihu (Lev. 10:1-7) The tabernacle was erected and consecrated and its ministry begun, when the first thing we see is the failure of man. The sons of Aaron offer "strange fire" to God and are immediately struck dead. Verse 3 explains: "This is it that the LORD spake, saying, I will be sanctified in them that come nigh me." In other words, God demands that He "be treated as holy by those who come near" to Him.

What had they done wrong? They were to take coals from the brazen altar at the gate of the tabernacle, to place on incense they presented to Yahweh at the golden altar in the holy place. They improvised and brought foreign fire from some place other than the brazen altar. Men can only approach a holy God on the basis of atonement. No worship, prayer or service is acceptable on any other basis, for God is HOLY and is to be recognized as such.

Moses and the rock (Num. 20:7-12). When Israel murmured for water the LORD again made provision by giving water from a rock as previously in their journey. But this time Moses was to speak to the rock rather than smite it as before. Moses, in frustration and anger, smote the rock twice and denounced the people's rebellion. Water was graciously given, but Moses was rebuked and told he could not enter the promised land. Why? "Because ye believed me not, to sanctify me [treat me as holy] in the eyes of the children of Israel." The greatest sin a minister of God can commit is to misrepresent the character of God. GOD WILL NOT NEGOTIATE HIS CHARACTER.

Uzza and the ark (I Chron. 13) David wanted to enthrone Yahweh in his new capital of Jerusalem. Unfortunately he used a Philistine method of transporting the ark of God, a cart pulled by oxen. When the procession reached the threshingfloor of Chidon the cart was shaken and the ark looked as if it would fall off. Uzza sprang to the rescue and took hold of the ark, and the LORD struck him dead. David's religious parade came to a halt, and he was afraid.

David went home and did some Bible homework and discovered that the Law clearly stipulated that the ark was not to be touched and was to be transported by the Kohathites with poles placed through rings on the sides of the ark. He instructed the Levites accordingly (15:2) and did it the second time according to "the due order" (15:13).

We may wonder why such drastic measures on God's part. The LORD was making it very plain at the commencement of the

Davidic reign that the standards had not been lowered, the covenant was still in effect, God was still holy. The hand of a man defiled the ark more than the dirt on the road.

Christ and His Cross (Psa. 22:1-6) David cried in anguish of soul, "My God, my God, why hast thou forsaken me?" Why was God so deaf to his prayer? Verse 3 states: "But thou are holy, O thou that inhabitest the praises of Israel." He knew a holy God could only do right. David therefore submitted to His holy God in worship.

The Son of David cried these same words out of the darkness of Calvary (Matt. 27:46). Why would the spotless Son of God be forsaken by His Father? The answer: "Thou art holy." The Son was bearing the sins of His people on the cross, and He submitted to the wrath of a holy God in obedience as a penal substitution.

Spurgeon writes:

> However ill things may look, there is no ill in thee, O God! We are very apt to think and speak harshly of God when we are under his afflicting hand, but not so the obedient Son. He knows too well his Father's goodness to let outward circumstances libel his character. There is no unrighteousness with the God of Jacob, he deserves no censure; let him do what he will, he is to be praised, and to reign enthroned amid the songs of his chosen people.[9]

In the light of the above truths, here are a couple of considerations to ponder:

- Can we hope to escape God's wrath with all our sins, when God spared not His sinless Son when bearing His people's sins?
- Are we sure we understand how a sinner can be right with such a holy God?

We must be sure we are not by-passing God's one righteous provision for the sinner's salvation in the work of His Son (Acts 4:12). Is it not possible for us to offer "strange fire"?

How about our worship? Does it emphasize the way in which we appear before men, or is it solemnly concerned with how we appear to God? Does it tend to secularize the sacred and profane the holy to bring it down to man's level? Does it have a tendency to make Christianity merely acceptable to non-believers?

We are living with the fruits of the baby-boomer generation. It is a consumer oriented generation, and they look at the church just like they look at a salad bar or a supermarket. The effort today is to try to appeal to this consumer generation. There are baby boomers who will send their children to one church and they themselves go to another. They are always looking for the church with a better program. There is no commitment—only a "what-can-I-get-out-of-it" attitude.

The Word of God says, however, that if baby boomers do not repent of their sins of selfishness, self-righteousness, and self-sufficiency, they are going to die and go to hell. We are not going to help them by lowering the standards of God in order to get them into our churches.

Is our worship Christ-like? In the light of who God is and what kind of God He is, how should we worship Him?

In Matthew 6:9 we have the Lord's Prayer. Notice the first petition: "After this manner therefore pray ye: Our Father which art in heaven, Hallowed be thy name."

Above everything else we ever would ask of God, the first prayer we should pray is, "Lord, let your name be Holy." If that is not our goal, if that is not our consuming passion, then forget about "forgive me my sins." Forget about "my daily bread." Forget about "deliver me from evil."

God, let Your name be Holy.

The God of Condescending Mercy

God is not just above and beyond His creation; Isaiah 57:15 also reveals God to be an immanent God, One Who is in His creation, active, even in condescending mercy to sinful men.

God's Mercy to Sinners

The Immanence of God

Immanence means God is in His creation. He is Creator and Sustainer (Col. 1:15-18; Heb. 1:2,3). God is separate from His creation (contrary to pantheism), but He is still in His creation, active in a number of ways (contrary to deism).

In Providence: Every believer is thankful for the God of providence, who makes all things work together for good for those called by Him and who love Him (Rom. 8:28).

In Salvation History: The Scriptures reveal the history of redemption from the Fall in Eden with its promise of the Seed of the woman (Gen. 3:15) to Israel, to Christ, to the Church, to the promise of the coming again of Christ, and to a future Kingdom of God. History is HIS-STORY.

In the Incarnation: The Creator, the Word (John 1:1), became flesh and dwelt among us (John 1:14). To see the incarnate God the Son is to see God the Father, for He reveals Him (John 1:18; 14:9).

In the Holy Spirit: Acts 2:1,2 records the Advent of the third

Person of the Trinity to be the element, indweller and enduer of the Church of Christ. This is the Age of the Holy Spirit.

As far as history is concerned, the classic world view was the one that saw God as transcendent and immanent. And there are links between the natural and the supernatural. God revealed Himself through creation and through His Word. Men could seek and find God. So there was interplay between the transcendent God and the world.

But then there came a time called the Enlightenment, just a very short little period of time, a little blip in history. Man began to see that the world was run by natural law, and he began to discover the so-called laws of nature. Science became more and more prominent, and man began to think: "We can get along here without God." So many relegated God to the transcendent and ruled Him out as a God of immanence.

We see in the early history of the United States that not every founder of our country was an evangelical Christian. Many of them were Deists, but they still had things in common with Christians. Though they ruled God out of running the universe (they said He just set up His laws and wound up the clock and let it run by itself), they still believed that there were links such as natural law and ethics. Emmanuel Kant thought he had destroyed all the classical arguments for the existence of God, but when he finished he let God in the backdoor, because he said that you can't have morality and ethics without God. And so our country was founded at least in the belief that you cannot have a society without ethics and morality.

When you cut off the transcendent from being a part of creation, sooner or later you come to what we have today, the secular world view in which there is a barrier between the transcendent and the creation. We can't know there is a God up there. All we know is how to run things down here by natural science and law. Therefore we are living our entire life in a secular age, which is a NOW age. We have philosophies that say, "You can't know anything unless you can feel it and taste it and touch it through empirical experience." Or, the existentialists say, "You're the most important one and you have got to find your own way and find yourself and do your own thing." This philosophy has permeated our entire society.

And then there is the very American philosophy called pragmatism. It's right if it works! If it doesn't work it's not right.

Because of the spiritual bankruptcy of secularism, efforts to bridge the supposedly uncrossable gap to the supernatural are being made today by occultism and New Age mysticism.

Sadly these philosophies have invaded the Church: existentialism (subjectivism, experience-self-centered), pragmatism (if it works, it is of God), and mysticism (by-passing the Word of God, experience centered, man deifying).

We send a missionary to a foreign country, and the first thing we expect him to do is learn the language. You and I today in our churches are in a foreign country. We are in a foreign culture. I believe that the average church does not even know the language, the language of how the people out there are thinking, because we are ignorant of our theology and our philosophy.

What is the REMEDY? A fresh vision of the God of the Bible!

The Incarnation of God

God's humble dwelling: He dwells in the high and holy place AND with the contrite and humble. Heaven is not too big for Him, and the human heart is not too small for Him.

God delights to dwell with His people. He walked with Adam and Eve in the cool of Eden's day before the Fall brought its terrible separation. He dwelt above the mercy seat in the Holy of holies of Moses' tabernacle in the midst of His redeemed people, Israel. Yahweh later took His abode in the Temple of Solomon. The Word became human and "tabernacled among us" (John 1:14), and Paul could speak of the mystery (revealed secret) of "Christ in you, the hope of glory" (Col. 1:27). Forever God will tabernacle with His saints in the New Jerusalem with a new heaven and a new earth (Rev. 21:1-3). He is a Tabernacling God.

God's humiliating descent: The heart of this *comfort* section of Isaiah's prophecy (Isa. 40-66) is the *Song of the Suffering Servant* (52:13-53:12), prophesying the sacrificial, substitutionary death of the Messiah. It points to the condescension of the Son of God in His humiliation to become a man, a servant, to be obedient unto the death of the Cross (Phil. 2:5-8).

The One Who so *humbled Himself* has been raised and exalted above every name, and at the Name of Jesus now every knee shall bow and confess Him as Lord (Phil. 2:9-11). The God-man Mediator is now the high and lofty One.

His humiliation means man's salvation:

> For ye know the grace of our Lord Jesus Christ, that, though he was rich, yet for your sakes he became poor, that ye through his poverty might be rich. (II Cor. 8:9)

Sinners Mourning over Sin

Isaiah describes a God Who revives (vs.15), heals (from sin's ills), leads (vs.18), and gives peace (vs. 19) to those who are "mourners" (vs. 18). Verse 15 describes them as the humble and contrite.

The Divine Reviving

> I dwell . . . with him also that is of a contrite and humble spirit, to revive the spirit of the humble, and to revive the heart of the contrite ones. (vs. 15)

The word *revive* translates the Hebrew verb *Chaya*, which is in a construction called the *Hiph'il*, meaning causative active. Thus the promise *is to keep alive*, or *restore to life*.

Therefore the promise of God through Isaiah to Israel is that

Yahweh will preserve the nation and restore them to covenant fellowship upon the condition of true repentance.

The God of mercy will save the repentant sinner and will revive a repentant Church as well.

The Sinner's Repentance

Biblical promise. The promise is for the "mourners" (vs. 18). Our Lord Jesus Christ made the same promise of blessedness:

> Blessed are the poor in spirit: for theirs is the kingdom of heaven. Blessed are they that mourn: for they shall be comforted. (Matt. 5:3,4)

James echoes Jesus' words in his *Ten Commandments of Revival* (4:7-11):

> Be afflicted, and mourn, and weep: let your laughter be turned to mourning, and your joy to heaviness. (vs. 9)

Of course affliction, mourning, and weeping are all biblical descriptions of repentance. It is mourning over sin, not just over its consequences, but because sin is against a holy God.

The reviving is for the contrite, the broken before God, and the humble, the lowly one. The promise of forgiveness and revival is always the same:

> If my people, which are called by my name, shall humble themselves, and pray, and seek my face, and turn from their wicked ways; then will I hear from heaven, and will forgive their sin, and will heal their land. (II Chron. 7:14)

Biblical precedent. Isaiah knew of what he was speaking by experience. He illustrates the truth of Isa. 57:15. In Isaiah 6 the prophet saw a vision of Adonay Yahweh, high and lifted up on His heavenly throne. He saw the seraphim before Him, crying, "Holy, holy, holy" (vss. 1-4). This vision of the transcendent holiness of

God resulted in a true vision of himself, for he cried out, "Woe is me! for I am undone; because I am a man of unclean lips, and I dwell in the midst of a people of unclean lips: for mine eyes have seen the King, the LORD of hosts" (vs. 5). It is only after we see who and what God is that we can see who and what we are.

From the "woe" of condemnation pronounced upon himself, the vision moved to the "lo" of forgiveness via atonement, for one of the seraphs took a coal off the altar (the place of atonement) and placed it upon Isaiah's lips with a pronouncement of cleansing: "Lo, this hath touched thy lips; and thine iniquity is taken away, and thy sin purged" (vss. 6, 7). This was no "strange fire" in this case. The prophet was clean in the sight of a holy God.

Then came the "go" of commission to that people of unclean lips from the Trinity (vs. 10ff).

David also illustrates this blessed truth in his repentance and restoration from his terrible sin with Bathsheba. In Psalm 51 we have the record of his prayer of confession and repentance. In verses 15-17 we hear his words:

> O Lord, open thou my lips; and my mouth shall shew forth thy praise [cf. Isa. 57:19—"I create the fruit of the lips"]. For thou desirest not sacrifice; else would I give it: thou delightest not in burnt offering. The sacrifices of God are a broken spirit: a broken and a contrite heart, O God, thou wilt not despise.

What is David doing here? He said, I can't go to the tabernacle and offer a sacrifice. He realized that even in the Old Testament God did not delight in the sense of accepting those as real atonements. They were only symbolic and prophetic. So what did David do? He came, completely throwing himself on the mercy of God, and saying, "God, I know your heart, and I'm trusting your heart, and I am trusting that you are a wise enough God to forgive and restore me even though I cannot come in any other way."

He said that a broken and a contrite heart, as far as God is concerned, is just like having an offering He accepts.

How did the heart of God respond? When God looked at David, He said, "Yes, I have a wise way, my heart has provided a way to forgive you. There is One coming, My Son, who is going to offer the sacrifice, who is going to make the atonement which you need." Therefore as we see in Romans 3:25,26, God passed over the sin of David. When Jesus died on the cross, He declared God to be righteous in forgiving David.

Biblical penitents. Job cried out of his sufferings for an audience with God. Though he was not suffering for his sins, he began to sin in his sufferings by his attitude. When God came on the scene, however, revealing Himself as the Creator and sovereign God of providence, Job had a different response:

> Behold, I am vile; what shall I answer thee? I will lay mine hand upon my mouth (Job 40:4).

> I have heard of thee by the hearing of the ear: but now mine eye seeth thee. Wherefore I abhor myself, and repent in dust and ashes (Job 42:5,6).

Simon Peter and his fishing partners had fished all night to no avail. After using Peter's boat from which to teach the people, Jesus told Simon to launch his boat out into the deep and let down his nets for fish. Skeptical, yet submissive, Simon obeyed, and the fish of Galilee rushed into his net, causing Peter to call on his partners for help, resulting in two boats full of catch (Luke 5:1-7). Verse 8 states:

> When Simon Peter saw it, he fell down at Jesus' knees, saying, Depart from me; for I am a sinful man, O Lord.

Jesus did not depart, but instead commissioned him: "And Jesus said unto Simon, Fear not; from henceforth thou shalt catch men" (vs. 10).

There is a direct relation between the distance or nearness of God and the hardness or brokenness of our hearts. Adam, after the Fall, hid from God, terrified at His presence. So it is with all of Adam's fallen sons. If men think that God may be anywhere around, they will make a wide detour around that place. This is why we do not find them in our churches, where any semblance of God's presence may be known. Though we do find them in our churches as professed members, when our assemblies are dead and devoid of His manifest presence.

But God in His sovereign grace will step into a sinner's life and make him face the reality of His presence. Our reaction is either to flee as Adam did or desire Him to leave as Peter did. The problem is that we cannot remain in His presence with our sin. The choice is to leave with our sin, or remain and let Him remove our sin. The safest place in all the universe for a sinner is in the presence of God. He will crush our hearts in His conquering grace. All our accomplishments and merits will lie smashed; all that will be left is CHRIST! There a holy God may dwell! O. Hallesby writes:

Why does God feel at home in your broken and contrite heart?

Because only the contrite heart can honor and worship the cross and the Crucified One. Only a contrite heart can admit that God is right in the crushing judgment which His cross passed upon the race as a whole and upon the individual. And only a contrite heart can acknowledge that God has a right to impart the unfathomable grace of the cross, and let the grace of God be what it is and reveal itself in all its fullness.

My broken-hearted and contrite friend! We cannot honor God more than by believing His grace. It is for this reason that He makes us contrite of heart.[10]

The Road to Revival

Christian, seek the transcendent, majestic, exalted Lord. "Draw nigh to God, and he will draw nigh to you" (Jam. 4:8). When God is distant, our hearts are hard. When He draws nigh, our hearts will be broken. We will see our own sin, confess and plead His mercy. He will hear from heaven and forgive our sin and heal. Grace is like water, it flows to the lowest level (Psa. 138:6; Jam. 4:6). He will cause us to live, dwell with us in fellowship, create lips of praise to Him. The greatest need in our day is for God to come down (Isa. 64:1,2) and dwell in His manifest holy presence in our churches again.

Dear reader, if you have never known the Lord Jesus Christ in saving grace, come to Christ as a beggar (poor in spirit), turn from your own righteousness as well as your sins and plead the mercy of a God Who gave His Son to die for sinners just like you.

> Nothing, either great or small,
>   Nothing sinner, no.
> Jesus died and paid it all,
>   Long, long ago.
>
> When He, from His lofty throne,
>   Stooped in love to die,
> Everything was fully done;
>   Hearken to His cry.

Weary, working, burdened one,
    Wherefore toil ye so?
Cease your doing, all was done,
    Long, long ago.

'Till to Jesus' work you cling
    By a simple faith.
"Doing" is a deadly thing,
    "Doing" ends in death.

Cast your deadly doing down,
    Down at Jesus' feet;
Stand "in Him," in Him alone,
    Gloriously complete.

It is finished, yes indeed,
    Finished every jot.
Sinner, this is all you need,
    Tell me, is it not?

—James Porter

END NOTES

1. John Seel, *The Evangelical Forfeit: Can We Recover?* (Grand Rapids: Baker Book House, 1933).

2. Ed Dobson, quoted by Seel, p. 114.

3. Seel, pp. 14,15.

4. George Marsden, quoted by Seel, p. 15.

5. Seel, p. 15.

6. (Grand Rapids: William B. Eerdmans Publishing Co.).

7. Seel, p. 27

8. H. C. Leupold, *Exposition of Isaiah*, 2 Vol. in 1 (Grand Rapids: Baker Book House, 1971), 2:279.

9. Charles H. Spurgeon, *The Treasury of David*, 7 Vols. in 2 (Byron Center, MI: Associated Publishers and Authors, Inc., 1970), 1:369.

10. O. Hallesby, *Religion or Christian?* (Minneapolis: Augsburg Publishing House, 1939), p. 170.

Missionary Classics

James Stewart, Missionary
by Ruth Stewart Fajfr

William Chalmers Burns
and Robert Murray McCheyne
(Combined)
by James A. Stewart

Man in a Hurry
by James A. Stewart

Praying Hyde
Edited by Capt. E. G. Carré

Booklets with a Ministry

Almost . . . But Lost
by Carolyn Reno

Redeemed:
Counsel for New Christians
by James A. Stewart

She was Only 22
by James A. Stewart

Evangelicals and the W.C.C.
by James A. Stewart

Order from:
Revival Literature
P. O. Box 6068 • Asheville, NC 28816

1-800-252-8896

www.revivallit.org

Other Christ-exalting and Soul-searching Titles by
Revival Literature

Healing for the Mind

The Shepherd and His Sheep

Roman's Road of Grace

Gospel Missions

Lordship of Christ

Call to the Ministry

The Narrative

Still Waters

Pastures of Tender Grass

Drops from the Honeycombs

Evangelism

Evangelism Without Apology

Heaven's Throne Gift

The Heavenly Executive

Come, O Breath

The Wonder of God's Tomorrow

Reproductions

Opened Windows

The Phenomena of Pentecost

The Fire of God

Rent Heavens

Spurgeon, Glorious Spurgeon

Our Beloved Jock

I Must Tell

James Stewart, Missionary

Our Heavenly Inheritance

Better Than Wine

Letters from Ruth

Revival Literature
P. O. Box 6068 • Asheville, NC 28816

1-800-252-8896

www.revivallit.org